F
StO

Stolz, Mary

Cat walk

DATE DUE

Quiz #   603
AR B.L.   4.3
Points   3.0   M G

CAT WALK

Other Novels by Mary Stolz

What Time of Night Is It?
Go and Catch a Flying Fish
Cider Days
Ferris Wheel
Cat in the Mirror
The Edge of Next Year
Lands End
Leap Before You Look
By the Highway Home
Juan
The Dragons of the Queen
A Wonderful, Terrible Time
Maximilian's World
The Noonday Friends
A Love, Or a Season
The Mystery of the Woods
The Bully of Barkham Street
Siri the Conquistador
Who Wants Music on Monday?
Wait for Me, Michael
The Beautiful Friend
A Dog on Barkham Street
And Love Replied
Hospital Zone
Pray Love, Remember
Ready or Not
The Organdy Cupcakes
The Sea Gulls Woke Me
To Tell Your Love

MARY STOLZ
CAT WALK

with drawings by

ERIK BLEGVAD

1 8  1 7

———— HARPER & ROW, PUBLISHERS ————

Cambridge, Philadelphia, San Francisco, London, Mexico City, São Paulo, Sydney

———— NEW YORK ————

Cat Walk
Text copyright © 1983 by Mary Stolz
Illustrations copyright © 1983 by Erik Blegvad
Printed in
the United States of America. For information address
Harper & Row, Publishers, Inc., 10 East 53rd Street,
New York, N.Y. 10022. Published simultaneously in
Canada by Fitzhenry & Whiteside Limited, Toronto.

Library of Congress Cataloging in Publication Data
Stolz, Mary, date
    Cat walk.

    Summary: Yearning to be more than just a barnyard
rat catcher, a young cat in search of a name embarks
on a journey that finally leads him to a special place
he can call a home.
    [1. Cats—Fiction]   I. Blegvad, Erik, ill.
II. Title.
PZ7.S875854Cav 1983   [Fic]   82-47576
ISBN 0-06-025974-4
ISBN 0-06-025975-2 (lib. bdg.)

First Edition

For

JOHANNA & THOMAS STOLZ
KELSEY & EBEN SCHAEFER
MAGGIE & PAUL CARSON
With love & admiration

CAT WALK

"—so long as I get *somewhere*," Alice added as an explanation.

"Oh, you're sure to do that," said the Cat, "if you only walk long enough!"

from Alice's Adventures in Wonderland
by Lewis Carroll

A LITTER OF THREE KITTENS was born in the hayloft of a barn in Vermont on a June day
a while ago. A good place to be born. Snug.
Safe.

Sunlight came through a slatted window and
shone on the straw where these kittens lived with
their mother. Rain sounded like millions of tiny
bird claws on the roof. Or like drums beating. When
the moon coursed the sky, the straw turned silver.
Other times, at night, the barn was quite dark. But
always there were promising sounds that, when the
kittens were older and bigger, they could investigate. Scurryings. Squeakings.

Until they were three months old, any today was
like any yesterday for the kittens.

There was a gray kitten. And a tiger. And a black,
with the biggest paws his mother had ever seen.
Six toes on each foot. Front and back. As he grew,
his feet grew with him. They were white. He looked
like a black kitten who took a daily walk through
a dish of whipped cream.

3

They played, they slept, they drank their mother's milk. After a while they began to catch the odd mouse. In a little while further still, they were finding their own food, up there in the hayloft, and their mother paid them less attention.

No more being held down with a firm paw while she washed their ears and bottoms. No more snuggling close to her belly to feed and fall asleep.

The kittens didn't mind. They were busy growing.

The time came when, at night, their mother went down a long wooden ladder to the barn floor, slid under the door where a hole had been worn away, and disappeared until dawn. Her kittens stayed in the hayloft and didn't dream of change.

They became aware that creatures besides cats existed. On the barn floor chickens wandered in and out all day. In the morning, even before the songbirds stirred, the farm rooster crowed the day awake. On the highest beam in the barn, a little screech owl slept. Outside, in the eaves, swallows nested.

Their mother told them what these creatures were called. She told them about farm animals they hadn't seen yet. Pigs that lived in a stone sty. Sheep that wandered a meadow beyond the barn. She told them how, in a pasture at the other side of the

farmhouse, two horses moved about cropping grass. Sometimes, she said, the farmer's daughters rode on their backs. She told of ducks on a pond out of sight behind the pasture. She told them that that huge chicken who strutted among the smaller ones down there was not a chicken at all. He was a turkey.

"*He* has a nasty surprise coming," said the cat mother. She added, "So have the rest of them. Except the horses and the rooster."

"What surprise?" asked the tiger kitten.

"Oh, well," said her mother. "It doesn't matter."

In time, they guessed. All animals know about death. But they don't think about it.

*   *   *

"Tell us about the farmer and the farmer's daughters," said the black kitten.

"They are human beings. They live in a big house at the other side of the garden. We have nothing to do with them."

"Why not?"

"They have their place, and we have ours."

"Is the barn ours?" the kittens asked.

"In a manner of speaking. It belongs to them because they own it. It belongs to us because we live and work here, and keep it tidy."

A mouse would know what she meant by that.

"Why do we have nothing to do with them?" the black kitten persisted. "They look nice. Anyway, one of them does."

"We are barn cats," the mother said. "We are wild. We have no names. We *never* go into houses. We are let live here, without nasty surprises, only because we work hard. Shall I tell you what happens to litters of *house* kittens that happen not to be wanted because they don't work?"

"You did tell us," said the tiger kitten, smallest and fiercest of the litter.

Her mother cuffed her ear. "Well, remember," she said.

Their mother instructed her kittens to learn the speech of human beings.

"Don't let people know you know what they're saying," said the mother cat. "Just listen."

"Why?" said the gray kitten, the biggest and shyest of the three.

"You can't tell what humans are up to until you hear what they say."

"That's funny," said the black kitten.

They all knew what other animals had in mind before a word was spoken. The border collie, Juniper, for instance. He didn't have to bark it for them to know that what he had in mind was to chase any barn cat that would run from him. Some ran, and some did not.

Juniper was one reason for staying in the hayloft until they were big. Anyway, bigger.

Juniper had his name. Juniper. The two horses, Claro and Quiz, had theirs. But the pigs, the sheep, the chickens, the ducks, and that turkey no more had names than the stones in a stream.

"Why don't they give *us* names?" the black kitten with the enormous white feet asked his mother.

An animal couldn't give himself a name, or pick one up from the barn floor. His mother wouldn't give him one. The gray and the tiger kittens said he was silly, but he did think it would be fine to have a name of his own.

"Only pets are given names," his mother explained. "We are not pets. We'll hear no more about it."

So far as she was concerned, that was that.

BECAUSE YOU DON'T talk about a thing does not mean you don't think about the thing.

The black kitten could not understand why his mother, his brother, and his fierce little sister did not see that names were important. Not to be "one of those barn cats," but to be—well, maybe . . . maybe Fluffy. He did have these enormous fluffy paws.

He imagined that the farmer's daughter, the one he liked to look at, would be good at names for cats.

"Don't those people in the house like cats?" he asked his mother.

"They like us fine. In our place. Which is here, working the barn and the yard."

"When are we going downstairs?" the tiger kitten demanded. "I'm tired of this hayloft."

The mother cat looked over her three children. The gray was shy, but so big that Juniper would let him alone. The tiger was small, but so fierce that Juniper would let her alone. The one she was uncertain about was that black with the feet. Not as big as his brother, but big enough. Not nearly so fearless as his sister. Fanciful. That's what he was. She had never had a kitten like him before. Dreaming about having a name, like some housebroken tabby. Dreaming, she was sure, about being a pet. Living in the farmhouse.

Juniper could catch that one easily and that would be the end of him, big feet, fancies, and all.

"You two," she said, indicating the tiger and the gray. "You come down with me today and I'll show you where the best hunting is. But you . . ." She looked at her odd third child. "You will remain up here."

"Why?" he asked.

"You're too dreamy. A chicken could beat you up while you were mooning over the farmer's daughter. Or the farmer's house."

The kittens never argued with their mother. While his sister and brother followed her down the ladder (not going facefirst and fast as she did, but backward and swinging from rung to rung), the black kitten leaned over the edge of the loft and watched.

Once on the floor way down there, the two kittens leaped in the air and scampered toward the great open door, scattering straw dust, tumbling each other, looking crazily free as they raced into the sunny yard and disappeared.

The big-footed cat settled where he was, eyes half closed. He was so quiet that a mouse came tunneling through the straw and popped out practically beside him. With a frantic scratching of tiny claws it turned and dove back.

The kitten didn't stir, though he knew what had taken place.

Unlike the rest of his family, he never caught a mouse unless he was hungry, and didn't enjoy it then. His mother, his sister, and even his shy brother were powerful mousers, and now they were all out there going about their trade.

He did not think it was his.

The farmer's daughters came into the barn, arguing.

"Oh, you are so *soppy*," said the bigger one. She was brown from the sun, scratched from brambles, scabbed from playing ball with neighboring boys. Her dark hair was cut short and her clothes were ragged from rough wear.

Her name, the kitten knew from having listened, was Kim.

"Soppy, soppy, soppy—that's what you are."

"Just because I don't want to swim in a dirty

brook with leeches in it," said the one whose name was Missy.

"You don't want to do anything. You don't want to play softball or climb trees or ride bikes—"

"I ride Quiz every day."

"Like you wished he was an *armchair*," Kim said, and swung onto her bicycle and rode off.

"You're going to get typhoid, swimming in that brook!" Missy shouted.

"A lot you care!" Kim yelled over her shoulder.

Missy shrugged, put a hand on her bicycle, then turned from it and glanced up. Her eyes met the eyes of the black kitten, staring down.

Missy was neat and not tanned. She had long brown hair and smooth skin and a gentle manner, and she was the farmer's daughter that this kitten mooned over. The other one reminded him of his sister.

"Why, look at you up there," said Missy in a thrilling low voice. "Have you been watching us? I believe you have." She studied him for a moment, then walked slowly toward the ladder. "Would you scratch me if I came up there, you wild barn cat you?"

A rumble of purring came from the loft.

The girl put one foot on the ladder, climbed several rungs, and waited. A proper barn cat would

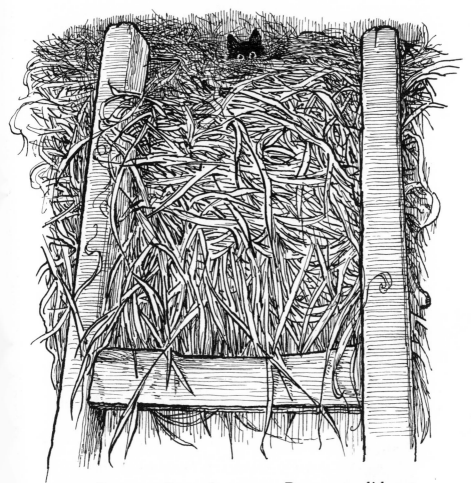

now disappear into the straw. Barn cats did not let human beings approach. It just was not done.

This barn cat waited to be approached.

After a while the girl continued climbing, until her face was on a level with the loft floor, several yards from where the cat crouched.

Again they waited.

She's afraid of me, thought the kitten. She's afraid of my teeth and the pins in my paws and my terrible reputation as a barn cat. He got up and very slowly, paw by paw by paw by paw, he walked toward her, purring.

Hours later, when the mother cat, followed by her two wild kittens, returned to the hayloft, the black kitten was nowhere to be found.

She searched everywhere, even climbing up on the barn beams, where the little screech owl chattered a threat.

"Have you seen my black kitten?" the mother cat demanded.

"I haven't seen anything. I've been asleep. Go away."

The kitten was not to be found.

"Stay here," said the mother cat to her wild children, and ran down the ladder to explore the yard and garden.

She had got closer to the farmhouse than she liked to be or had been before, when she saw the farmer's daughter (not the one brown as a field mouse; the other, who looked like a glass of Guernsey milk) coming down the walk pushing a doll carriage, leaning over and crooning into it.

"There's my Tootsy-Wootsy," she sang softly.

"My Bootsy-Wootsy darling. Oh, you little angel-pooh, you. I *must* pick you up."

She leaned over the buggy and lifted out the occupant, holding it close. The mother cat, watching, slowly blinked her eyes.

There he was, her peculiar son, lolling in the girl's arms, waving his tail dreamily. He wore a frilly yellow dress and a frilly yellow bonnet tied with a ribbon under his chin.

*   *   *

After a moment, the big cat turned and trotted back to the barn, ran up the ladder to the hayloft.

"Did you find him?" asked her two remaining kittens.

"Yes."

"Why isn't he with you?"

"Because he's lost."

"How can he be lost if you found him?"

"There are ways," said the mother cat. "Your brother has found one."

KIM, SPEEDING AROUND the corner on her bike, braked to a stop.

"What the heck are you doing now?" she asked her sister. She peered at the small face in the big bonnet. "Wow! Isn't that one of the barn cats? What'd you do, dope it?"

"He *came* to me."

"How long do you suppose he'll put up with being dressed in baby clothes?" Kim asked.

"He loves it," Missy said firmly. "Listen to him purr."

"And the first time he gets loose, that'll be the last you see of him. No self-respecting cat wou—"

"He isn't going to get loose. I'm going to keep him in the house. We're going to have a house cat, so there." She squeezed the black cat, who gasped and then resumed purring.

"Does he have to dress up like that indoors, too?"

"When I want him to. He's going to be my cat and do just what I want."

"Oh boy."

"What does that mean?"

Kim lifted her shoulders. "Only oh boy. What's his name?"

"Tootsy-Wootsy. Because he's got these absolutely enormous white tootsies."

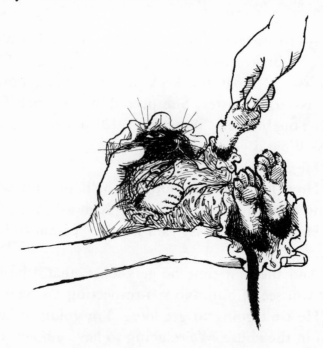

Kim looked closer. "Six toes for each foot. I've never seen that before. But it's a dumb name, and I wouldn't have a cat on a bet that liked wearing baby clothes."

"For goodness' sakes," said their mother, coming

out on the porch. "What's going on? Is that a cat, Missy?"

She came down the steps, studied Tootsy-Wootsy, lying back contentedly in Missy's arms. "I declare, one of the barn cats."

"I expect his mother will come looking for him," said Kim. "Probably, Missy, you've *broken* some poor mother's heart."

Missy looked away, but their mother said, "Don't you believe it. She's probably pleased as punch to have him gone. Animals know how to treat children. Get rid of them as fast as possible."

Neither girl looked alarmed at these words, but Tootsy-Wootsy stirred. *Was* his mother glad to get rid of him? He'd seen her a while ago, lurking in the larkspur, watching him.

She hadn't called to him, or made an effort to lure him from Missy's arms. So. She *was* glad to have him gone. He damped down a spurt of sadness. If she was glad, then so was he.

So there.

He was going to live in a house and have a name and wear pretty clothes. So very *there.*

That afternoon he was bundled into a box and driven, without a stitch on him, to a horrible place called the veterinarian's. There he was put on a cold table, with the veterinarian and the farmer's wife staring down at him.

"Fine little fellow," said the veterinarian, holding him this way and that, poking, prodding, peering. "Give me a dog anytime. I mean, you never know where you stand with a cat, do you? But this fellow kinda grabs me. I have *never* seen feet like that on a cat before. A bobcat, maybe. So, let's see. Ear mites, fleas, probably worms, but on the whole okay. We'll get him fixed up." He laughed. "Tip to tail, as you say."

The cat was subjected to dippage, swabbage, to needles and pills, to a bath. The next day, as he lay in his cage dreaming of his mother and the hayloft, longing for his brother and even his sassy sister, the farmer's wife and Missy returned for him.

Free of fleas and a few other things, he was driven back to the farm to begin life as a house cat.

It was blissful.

There were no mice in the house, but somebody was catching cans of food for him. Canned food was cooked, quite different from mouse. He liked it.

Except for his daily ride in the doll carriage, he couldn't get out of the house.

He had a litter pan in the bathroom. He slept on Missy's bed or on any of the furniture he wished to.

Everybody—even Kim, even Juniper—liked him.

Juniper played with Tootsy-Wootsy by the hour, and sometimes they slept together, which the kitten, growing to be a good-sized cat, liked better than sleeping with Missy.

Juniper's rough fur put him in mind of his moth-

er's soft coat. He liked the beating of Juniper's heart vibrating through his own body.

He didn't count all the reasons, but he was happy with Juniper.

And, for a while, he was pretty happy with his wardrobe.

Missy didn't keep him in clothes all the time. But no day passed that he was not outfitted for an hour or so in ruffly frocks, rompers, sunsuits, caps, bonnets. As the weather grew colder, he got to wear booties, personally knitted for him by Missy. She made him a pink sweater and a matching pink wool helmet that buttoned under his chin, and a pair of grape-colored leggings with a convenient hole for his tail to swing out of.

Missy called it his ski outfit.

He got to ride in the doll carriage every day.

"Every *day*," he said to Juniper one stormy autumn morning. "I'm not complaining, but every *day*?"

"I'd be complaining," said Juniper. "She tried that on me, when I was a puppy. Put a T-shirt on me that had *I Love a Dog's Life* printed on the front of it. I soon showed her."

"How?" Tootsy-Wootsy asked curiously.

"Growled. Tore at the thing with my teeth."

"I wonder they didn't get mad at you. Once when I didn't really feel like going for a ride in my ski outfit, I tried just the tiniest scratch on her hand. The littlest scratch you can image. And oh my, it was terrible. She yelled and her mother yelled and Kim laughed and the farmer said any more of that and it was back to the vet's for me. For *keeps*, he said. Then I suppose I'd have to live in that cage, forever being dipped for fleas and stuck with needles and all the stuff that veterinarian does to animals."

"Maybe yes, maybe no," said Juniper.

"What does that mean?"

"Let it pass," Juniper answered. "Anyway, don't scratch her anymore and you'll be fine."

"But why did they let you growl and tear your clothes and they won't let me give a teeny little scratch? Not to hurt. Just to show my wishes. I mean, Juniper, if they won't understand our language, how can we let them know how we feel?"

"It isn't how you feel that matters, it's how you behave."

"But you—"

"I work. I herd the sheep. When we have cattle, I drive the cows out to the meadow in the morning and back to barn at dusk. The farmer wasn't going to lose a fine work dog like me just because some kid wanted to make a baby out of him. From the beginning," Juniper said smugly, "they knew I was going to be the best dog they ever had."

"Why can't I be the best cat they ever had?"

"Farmers like animals that *do* something for them. Like herding sheep. Or laying eggs. Or catching rats. Or turning into hams. All you do is lie around looking well dressed."

Tootsy-Wootsy had a mind to stalk off.

But he and Juniper were so comfortable here by the wood stove in the kitchen. Rain rattled against the windows and the wind whirled around the house. Tootsy-Wootsy thought about his family, probably sleeping in the cold straw. He thought about Quiz and Claro, and those sheep, standing in the meadow getting drenched. He thought of the pigs grunting in their damp stone house.

Wearing a ski outfit, even riding in a doll buggy that was getting awfully small, was no price to pay for being a warm and sheltered house cat, safe from the storm.

Well. A small price.

W INTER.
     The land lay under a shawl of snow.
     Air cold and clear as glass, darkening
now toward dusk. From the farmhouse chimney
smoke rose like a tall tree. And all the animals except Tootsy-Wootsy were out in the frigid day.

There were fewer of them now. The sheep had
disappeared. The pigs, having made hogs of themselves, were gone. And so was the turkey. But the
two horses raced about like colts, their breath
gauzy. The rooster, looking finicky, stalked about
the yard lifting his legs high. Juniper was walking
fence lines with the farmer.

The barn cats—well, they might be anywhere.

All animals, free and dressed in nothing but their
own feathers or fur, were out there, while Tootsy-
Wootsy walked up and down the hallway, lashing
his tail.

He was wearing his ski outfit, too small for him
now. Missy had got him dressed, so as to give him

an airing in the doll carriage, but then she'd gone off to have an argument with Kim and forgotten about him.

Now that he was a full-grown cat, she was not as attentive as she had been when he was small. But still she would not let him go outdoors except when she took him for rides.

"Why not just jump out of the buggy?" Juniper had asked.

"Dressed like this?" Tootsy-Wootsy moaned.

"Hmm. I see."

"Besides, ever since the day I *tried* to jump out, she puts me in this—this yellow sack thing that zips right up to my chin. I can't jump in that thing. I can hardly move."

"Yes. I see."

No, you don't, thought Tootsy-Wootsy. You don't know what it's like to be in a sack unless you've been in one.

Now, half listening to the two girls having a hand-to-hand difference of opinion in the living room, he tried with his teeth to pull the leggings off. Hopeless. He went after the booties, and after a long time succeeded in dragging off the one on his right front foot.

Encouraged, he started on the left front foot.

*   *   *

Pummeling each other, the two girls rolled across the rug. Their grandmother looked up from the book she was reading, watched for a while, and then said, "You ought not to do that."

"Why not?" said Missy, pulling her sister's hair.

"What's *ought*?" gasped Kim, punching Missy on the shoulder. "What's *ought* got to do with anything?"

"Ought implies what is seemly. Becoming. You *ought*, for instance, to listen to your grandmother, because she's a frail old lady."

Kim yelled with laughter, then yelped as Missy tried to bite her. "You aren't a frail old lady. Daddy says you're tough as old boots. Biting is *not* fair, Missy. . . ."

Juniper, who really was tough as old boots, sat beside the grandmother, watching with interest. He regarded the two girls' frequent combats as a game they played. In real fights—he'd been in a few—there was no nonsense about "fair."

"Well then," said the grandmother, not lifting her voice, "you ought to listen to me because I am the Great Ought." She returned to her book.

Kim and Missy sat up.

"Since *when* have you been the Great Ought?" Kim asked, giggling.

"Since your father was a little boy. *He* knew an Ought when it looked him in the eye. But Oughts don't have the power they had when I was a child. *My* father, now. There was an Ought for you. No back talk or biting when he said what ought or ought not to be done. So . . . what is the argument about this time?"

But neither girl could remember.

"Then I suggest that you go and ride Claro and Quiz. It's going to rain later in the day."

They did not ask how she knew. She knew just about everything.

"Let's go," said Kim, and they went out the back door, Missy quite forgetting Tootsy-Wootsy in the hall. The second front bootie was tied tighter than the one he'd got off. He abandoned it and started, with his free foot, to try pulling the knitted helmet over his head. It wouldn't come.

Inside him, rage that had simmered for a long time rose all at once like milk boiling over. At that precise scalding moment, the farmer's wife came in the front door with a friend.

Tootsy-Wootsy shot out between their legs and raced down the long drive toward the highway.

He heard the farmer's wife cry out, "Oh, my goodness . . . I *knew* this would happen some-time," and the friend's question, "What *was* that?"

Then he was out of earshot, racing toward he knew not what. He only knew what from, and kept going.

A driver coming down the icy road suddenly stared, stepped on the brake, avoided hitting what he did not believe he saw—a cat dressed for skiing— and slid into a snowbank, where he came gently to rest against a tree.

*   *   *

Tootsy-Wootsy, who had never before in his life been frightened, bolted across the highway in total panic. The car coming toward him, the shriek of the brakes, a truck coming along behind it, lent him speed. Leaping a ditch, streaking under a fence, he reached a field on the opposite side, where he crouched, trembling, in the cold-stiffened weeds.

Far too shaken to recross the road, he thought with frantic regret of all he had run away from. The warm stove. Food. Safety.

Juniper!

Without a thought, without a good-bye, he had run away from his friend, and was here in a vast and chilly meadow, cut off from the life he had known. And from his *friend.* He looked over his shoulder at the wide road, wondering if he dared recross it. But the traffic was increasing, roaring in both directions.

He could never do it.

He turned and looked ahead, across miles of frozen grass and snow.

In a little while, he started walking, and only then noticed that in his scramble he had shed the two hind booties. This should have cheered him.

He was past being cheered.

He trudged on, finding the ground cold, the air cold, the darkening world very cold indeed.

Tootsy-wootsy knew to the minute when it was his suppertime.

It was suppertime *now*.

Only there was no kitchen, no bowl with CAT written at the bottom. No little girl to wait on him. In his memory, Missy was now all kindness and love. Everything had been done out of love for him. Dressing him up, trundling him about in that doll buggy, trapping him in that yellow sack that prevented him from escaping when all the other animals were free . . .

Free!

He had been walking for a long time, and now it was full dark and he was hungry and still wearing the ski suit that was too tight, and the helmet, and the one front bootie that he could not get off.

But he was a free cat.

His spirits shifted upward. Ahead was a house, with yellow lights at the windows and the familiar sound of a dog's barking.

He was missing Juniper more acutely with each passing moment. Missing the shaggy coat, the doggy smell, the warm talky companionship of his good, his true, his only friend. No dog would ever take Juniper's place for him, but any dog was better than no dog at all to be close to.

This one had a voice that boomed like a storm in the hills, where Juniper's bark was more like bells, but a bark was a bark and meant dog, and Tootsy-Wootsy confidently ran toward it.

The next thing he knew, and he didn't remember getting there, he was clutching a tree branch while down below—not far enough down—this terrible huge animal was roaring and trying to knock the tree over.

From the house, a woman started calling to him, telling him to stop that racket, but the creature paid no attention. Just kept bounding and bellowing. Tootsy-Wootsy, faint with fear, with hunger, with cold, with wild regret for all he'd left behind him, dug in his claws and waited—for what, he knew not.

The woman, pulling on a sweater, came out of the house and made the dog, whose awful name was Soldier, be quiet.

"Stay!" she said to him. "Sit! What *is* up there in the tree?"

The monster sat, staring upward, tongue lolling, and the woman went away. Then she came back, with a man. Then a blinding light forced Tootsy-Wootsy to close his eyes.

He could not think. All memory of Juniper, the kitchen, his bowl with CAT on the bottom and chicken on top, disappeared. He was a small bundle of terror in pink and purple, treed by a superdog, trapped in torchlight.

He gave up hope.

At the bottom of the tree the man, the woman, and the dog were all looking up.

"At first I thought it was a *baby*," said the woman.

"How would a baby get up in our beech tree?"

"Why would a cat be dressed in ski clothes?"

"How should I know? The latest cat fad, maybe."

"Hand knitted. And it's lost three of its booties."

"You've lost all of yours. I'm going inside."

"What about the *cat*?"

"Let it take the next chair lift. Come along, Soldier." He stumped toward the house, turned, and said, "Mathilda Pursely, are you coming in or aren't you?"

With a last upward glance, Mrs. Pursley, too, turned away. She followed her husband and Soldier into the house, and pretty soon the lights went out.

Silence, except for the hoot of a hunting owl, folded over the world.

Tootsy-Wootsy decided to get out of this tree and away from this place. He loosened his grip on the branch, wriggled, and realized that he had no idea of what to do next.

Go forward? Go backward? Turn around? Just *drop*?

How did a cat who had never been up in a tree before get out of it? He thought of his mother. Had she given them instructions, back in those lovely hayloft days, about tree descent? She'd taught them so much, including the value of a tree if Juniper got too close.

He gazed into the dark that even his cat's eyes could scarcely penetrate, trying to remember. He supposed that his mother had supposed that her

kittens would know how to go up a tree, and also
how to come down one.

He didn't know. He didn't know how he'd got
up it, and didn't know how to get out of it.

It began to snow. Lightly at first. It soon quick-
ened to a heavy fall.

Timidly, Tootsy-Wootsy began to inch backward
along the bough. He knew he couldn't remain
where he was, with snow clotting the air and his
clothes stiffening. He stopped for a moment to try
once again to pull off the remaining bootie, slid
sideways, fell a couple of feet, and was caught on
a projecting branch.

He hung there, thrashing about, then all at once
plummeted to the ground, ski pants unraveling as
he dropped.

He picked himself up, glanced at the long grape-
colored yarn that dangled from a terribly high
branch. There was all that remained of his leggings.
And here he was, nearer to being free of his entire
attire.

Limping, as the bootie on his front foot was forming icicles, he plodded toward a big shape that
looked, in the rushing snow, sort of like a barn.

If he could get there, maybe he'd find a hayloft.
Maybe a mouse, if he could manage to catch one.
Even when he felt well, he was a poor mouser.

His footprints were huge and blurry in the snow

and soon covered over as he walked around the building looking for a way in.

There was one. A jagged ragged hole big enough for him to squeeze through.

Tootsy-Wootsy found that it was not a barn. Just a big cold place where a car and a truck were parked. No hayloft. Not a thing on the hard cement floor that offered a place to snuggle.

Tootsy-Wootsy's adventure had now been going on for hours. He was hungry, exhausted from all that walking, frightened, and terribly sleepy. Glancing around, his eyes now accustomed to the dark, he saw that the truck was the kind that Juniper rode in the back of when the farmer was driving over the field or into town.

With a weary feeling that being in the sort of place that Juniper was used to would give him comfort, he gave the last leap of which he was capable and landed in the back of the pickup.

There, in a corner, was a tarpaulin. Tootsy-Wootsy staggered to it, burrowed through its stiff cold folds, and fell asleep in his wet clothes.

"MORNING, MRS. PURSLEY," said Jerry, owner of Jerome's Service Station. "Fill 'er up?"

"And check under the hood. Have to use your phone if it isn't down from the storm, like ours."

"Nope. Go right ahead."

The snow had stopped falling, and road-clearing crews were out. Except for where they cut their paths, the world was softly covered, as if with a white feather comforter.

Tootsy-Wootsy, peering out from under the rumpled tarpaulin, blinked slowly. His vision was dazzled. He tested his muscles, wondering if he'd be able to move. He was.

He made sure no one was watching and jumped to the ground. The immediate thing was to find something to eat.

Catch it, or beg it, or find it by chance. He must eat.

* * *

Jerry, who'd been having his morning coffee and doughnuts when Mrs. Pursley drove in, had left these on a bench just inside the lubricating bay. It took Tootsy-Wootsy, assisted by his nose, no time at all to find the doughnuts, snatch one, and scamper with it out of sight under a car. There, purring furiously, he devoured every crumb.

He was starting out for seconds when Jerry walked over to get his coffee. He stared down at the paper plate, took off his glasses since he sometimes saw better without them, put them back on, glanced at Mrs. Pursley, shook his head, and shrugged.

"Would've sworn I had two left," he muttered, picking up the remaining doughnut and his coffee. "Beats all."

The pickup truck left. Other vehicles came in and went their way.

Tootsy-Wootsy remained under the car gnawing at his bootie because there was nothing else to do. He wished that Missy had knitted his clothes out of spaghetti. By now he could have eaten them off. He was fond of spaghetti, with butter and cheese on it especially.

The bootie string was chewed through. Almost carelessly, Tootsy-Wootsy pulled the bootie off. He was thinking he might go for the helmet next when a car was driven up next to his and parked. Tootsy-Wootsy, moving in a trance, crept from his dark lair and studied the automobile, from which there came a delicious wave of heat.

No one was paying attention to it. It had simply been left, tempting and unguarded. Tootsy-Wootsy leaped to the warm hood and settled down in ecstasy.

Things were busy at the service station, and it was some time before Jerry noticed, at the other end of the lot, something on the hood of Dr. Lakeland's Dodge. He strolled over, frowning, then stood looking down with a puzzled smile. He was a cat lover. No matter how they came, even partly dressed in wet bedraggled clothes, he was a man who liked cats.

He studied this one, so oddly costumed, so soundly asleep, then began gently to remove the ice-encrusted helmet.

Tootsy-Wootsy awoke at the man's touch, bristled, and immediately calmed when he realized that at last he was to be released from his tight, tormenting garments. He lay still, flopping his tail, gazing up at his rescuer.

"Ate my doughnut, I'll bet," said Jerry. "You're some little girl's pet, and you're lost, right? Or you ran away, maybe? And you're hungry, no maybe, right?"

Tootsy-Wootsy purred loudly.

"I'll see what I can do," said Jerry. He turned and called to his mechanic, "Clay, take my car and run over to the IGA, get a couple of cans of cat food." He looked at Tootsy-Wootsy. "Big cans," he added.

He picked the cat up, carried him into the office, which was littered and oily and dusty and warm. Sitting in a battered captain's chair, he held Tootsy-Wootsy on his lap.

"You're a fine boy," he said. "Just the kind of cat I'd like to have at home."

Tootsy-Wootsy butted his big head against the

big grimy hand and purred even more loudly.

"Can't be done," Jerry went on. "My boy's aller-
gic to cats." He hesitated, thinking, and sighed
hugely. "You wouldn't like living with him, anyway. Don't much like it myself. Ah, here's Clay
with your eats."

While Tootsy-Wootsy bolted half a can of beef
and liver dinner from an ashtray, Jerry and Clay
looked him over.

"Big, ain't he?" Clay said.

"Sure is. Got the biggest darn feet. Like a pu-
ma's."

"Whatcha gonna do with him, Jerry?"

"Well. I suppose he's some kid's pet. Come all
dolled up in a hat and sweater. Looked homemade."

"Huh?"

"Little girls do that. Dress up cats, or puppies,
and push them around in baby carriages. Maybe
this fellow got fed up. I took the stuff off him. He
was darn near froze into it. Look at him eat."

"Give him the other half a can."

"Not yet. Might make him sick. No telling when
he ate last, so we shouldn't overload his belly. I
never did see such *feet* on a cat before."

"What's his name, I wonder."

"Think I'll call him Snowshoes."

"You gonna keep him?"

"Don't see why he shouldn't live here at the station. Cat that size is probably a good ratter. Makes sense to keep him."

"Sure, Jerry. What rats?"

"I don't see any reason why I shouldn't have a cat here if I want one. No way of finding where he comes from. Is there?"

"No way at all," Clay said obligingly. "Snowshoes, huh? What about nights? You gonna—take him home with you?"

Jerry shook his head, not looking at Clay.

"He could stay in here, in the office."

Jerry considered. "It's warm, of course. And these nights are from the North Pole. Still. Suppose there was a fire or something? He couldn't get out. I know what—get that packing crate the hubcaps came in last week, Clay."

He reached under the counter and pulled out a pillow and an old army blanket. Once in a while, in a blizzard so bad that even he couldn't drive through it, Jerry put up a cot and slept here in the office. Last night hadn't qualified for these measures. To a Vermonter, that had been little more than a good dusting of powder.

On the other hand, he thought, for a cat—even a cat that came with snowshoes as standard equipment—it would've been impossible to get far. He must've stowed away in a car. Stood to reason.

"Stands to reason," he told Clay, as they placed

the packing crate against the outside office wall, out of the wind. "Probably he's a stowaway."

"How d'ya figure?"

"If he was riding around *with* somebody in that pure-awful getup, they'd have been calling around, trying to find him, right? So. Nobody's been asking."

"It's early yet."

Jerry scowled at his helper. "Probably somebody passing through. Won't recall at all where they stopped," he said, reversing himself.

Clay nodded agreement. One way or the other, it didn't matter to him.

He didn't ask why Snowshoes was going to be a garage cat instead of going home nights with Jerry. He knew the reason. Jerry and his wife, Ella, had a son, Roddy, who had been a nice little boy. They were hoping that one day he'd be a nice big boy. Meanwhile, in Clay's opinion, Roddy was as mean a nine-year-old kid as you'd find in all New England. Not the kind Jerry would bring a nice cat home to.

"A boa constrictor, now . . ." Clay muttered.

"What?" said Jerry.

"Oh, nothin'. Just talking to myself," said Clay as he slid under a station wagon.

JERRY, BY NATURE a good-humored party, spent
a pleasant day at his service station, gabbing
with Clay and his customers, filling tanks,
checking tire pressures, wiping windshields, and
in between times working on cars brought in for
his mechanic's attention.

Jerry enjoyed his work.

Today, he had the additional pleasure of finding
that Snowshoes took to him. Followed him around,
looked right in his eyes from time to time, and
meowed some message he couldn't altogether catch
but guessed was a message of gratitude for the res-
cue operation.

"That old boy really cottons to you, Jerry. Never
saw the like."

"He's not old," Jerry said to Clay, pleased but
not wanting to show it too much. "Not even a year,
I bet."

"If you say. Cats aren't my bag."

Toward closing time, Jerry's cheerful disposition

44

took a downward turn. It always did, when he had
to go home. It didn't bear thinking what Ella had
to put up with between the time school let out
and the hour—unpredictable—when they finally
got Roddy down for the night.

Since it didn't bear thinking of, he didn't think
of it. Not until five o'clock, six days a week. Sun-
days, when the station was closed, they all just got
through the day the best way they could.

It was dark by five o'clock. Clay had left, and
Jerry, after locking up, stopped by the packing crate
to explain matters to Snowshoes.

"You'll be fine in there," he said, looking with
approval at the cat, already settled snugly in the
blanket, which was rumpled on the pillow, forming
a cozy bivouac. "You had a whole can of cat food
today, so that'll hold you till morning. Maybe I'll
bring you some chicken gizzards tomorrow."

Basking in the warmth of Jerry's voice tones,
Snowshoes kneaded the rough blanket. The crate
seemed to throb with his husky purring.

"You see?" Jerry said to Clay a few days later.
"Ever since he came, we haven't seen a rat."

"We didn't see any before he came, Jerry."

"Doesn't prove anything, just because we didn't
see them. Now we *know* there aren't any."

"How?"

"Clay," Jerry said patiently, "we got this big cat here, and *no* rats. Right? That proves he's keeping them away."

"If you say so."

"Don't you like Snowshoes?"

"Oh, hey, Jerry. Don't get me wrong. I think he's a great old boy. Young fella. No, I really like having him around the place."

Whether Clay did or did not like him was of no interest to Snowshoes. His heart belonged to Jerry. He followed the big slow man around the station area all day, sitting on the platform where the pumps were while Jerry filled tanks, stalking after him, tail high, while he moved from air hose to office to lubricating bay. Sharing his lunch. Sharing his day.

Where Jerry was, there was Snowshoes.

"Make a lovely couple, you do," Clay observed.

Customers, of course, noticed the presence of the cat with the outsize paws. Snowshoes still could not resist a warm engine, and if a car was left toward closing time for attention in the morning, Snowshoes got on it and remained until the engine cooled. What with walking through melting snow, oil spills, sand, and dirt, he left his mark. Jerry didn't pay much attention until the fifth or sixth complaint.

"See here, Jerome," said Dr. Lakeland, "that animal of yours left footprints the size of frying pans on my hood again. Scares my wife silly. She insists there's a mountain lion loose in the hills. I keep telling her it's just a bobcat you've adopted. . . ."

After the doctor had gone, Jerry fixed serious eyes on Snowshoes, who gave a mute meow.

"That's *your* story," Jerry said. "We'll have to have a talk about this. If you'll just step into my office here. . . ."

He picked up the cat and carried him into the warm and littered little room, where for a while they sat, Snowshoes purring, Jerry humming, the radio rocking.

Clay stopped and looked in, grinning. "You give him what for, Boss?"

"We've reached an agreement. He goes on sitting on the hoods, and we wipe off the paw prints."

"Gotcha," said the ever-obliging Clay.

*   *   *

Weeks passed.

Spring stepped down on Vermont hills and pastures and as far away as New Hampshire and
Maine. She coaxed fiddler fern and skunk cabbage
to grow in the marshes; buds to bead along the
bough; bulbs to nose out of the earth; peepers to
begin their vespers.

Snowshoes, who had been living in a condition
of such loving contentment that he had almost—
never quite—forgotten Juniper, was napping on top
of his crate one afternoon when Roddy arrived.

Jerry had gone out to jump a stalled engine. When
he was away, Snowshoes lost interest in the activities of the station. Clay was kind enough, but not
a person Snowshoes could really take to. Aside from
Missy, whom he had liked in spite of a lot of things,
the only human being he had ever cared for was
Jerry. He did not like Jerry in spite of anything.
He loved him because of everything.

Snowshoes, lightly snoozing, became aware of a
strange voice addressing Clay.

"Where's my old man?"

"Your Dad's gone to jump a fellow's car," Clay
said stiffly. "I don't know when he'll be back, so
maybe there's no point waiting around," he added
in a hopeful tone.

"I'll wait if I wanna. You think you own this place?"

"I don't think you do."

"I'm gonna tell my father on you. I'll get you fired, see?"

"Ah—go grab some candy from a baby."

"Stupid old grease monkey."

This was said in a mutter as Roddy sauntered away from Clay, toward the side of the office.

He stopped.

Snowshoes sensed the halt, the intaken breath. He opened his eyes to slits and looked right into this boy's steady gaze.

"WELL, WELL," SAID RODDY. "So this's the cat everybody's talking about. Pretty scabby."

Snowshoes, who was in fact sleek and handsome, rippled back upon himself, fur lifting lightly. Turning his head warily, he took a quick look behind him and started off, but was seized in midair by strong grubby hands.

For the first time in his life, the cat lashed out. His hind feet with their long needly claws slashed the boy's arm.

Roddy, startled into fury, did not let go. Twisting Snowshoes around, he managed to get a tight grip on both front and back feet. He swung the snarling cat three times over his head, then flung him across the lot against a tractor. Snowshoes hit full force and fell to the ground, stunned, as Roddy, bleeding and enraged, advanced and kicked him several yards into the public telephone booth.

At that moment, Jerry drove into the station.

"What's happening here?" he shouted in a frightened voice. He grabbed his son by the shoulders.
"Roddy, what are you *doing*—"

"He *went* for me," Roddy sobbed. "He *attacked*.
Lookit me, bleeding all over. Lookit what he did
to me! I'm gonna tell Mama!"

"Listen. Look here, son. Come with me and I'll
hose your arm off. We better use soap. Cat scratches
can be dangerous—" He broke off, looking toward
Snowshoes, huddled in the phone booth.

"Who's important?" Roddy yelled. "Me or that
mangy dumb—"

"Come here, and I'll wash you off. Clay, we got
some Mercurochrome there in that first-aid kit. Get
it for me. Come on, son."Again he looked over his
shoulder at Snowshoes. "I can't understand it. He's
a—a real easygoing animal."

"He's a crazy cannibal. He tried to kill me. He
went for me, I tell you."

Jerry, over his son's head, looked at Clay, who
said, "Nope. Don't gimme that look, Jerry. You
asked. I wasn't gonna tell."

Jerry, with a sigh, tipped his son's chin up, looked
in his eyes. "You went for the cat, didn't you? For
no reason."

"I didn't! You gonna listen to that dopey Clay?"

"Roddy, why are you this way? Why do you *do*
things like this?"

"I don't know," said Roddy. He set his jaw bellig-erently. "Don't ask, cuz I don't know."

He was telling the truth.

He did not know why he did things like that. How should he know why?

Jerry pulled his son against him, held him, and said, "I wish you'd let me help you. Roddy, why don't you let us help you?"

For a moment the boy yielded to his father's voice and strong embrace. Then he pulled back, walked toward his bike, turned, and studied them. First Clay, then his father.

Last, he fixed a brooding gaze on Snowshoes, still in the phone booth with no idea of leaving until this menace was gone.

"I'll be back," said Roddy and pedaled slowly off, looking over his shoulder now and then, as if to fix everything in his mind.

Clay rubbed a hand across his mouth and chin, pushed his cap back, looked at his boss. "Gotta work on that squad car," he mumbled. "Told them I'd have it ready by three."

He left Jerry, who resettled his cap with a nervous jerk and walked across the lot to the telephone booth.

"Feel pretty bad, old boy?" said Jerry. He put a light hand on the cat's shoulder. Snowshoes winced. Shaking his head, exhaling a long shaky sigh, Jerry stooped and gently as possible put the cat in the truck, in the passenger seat.

"I'll run Snowshoes over to the vet's," he told Clay.

When he was on the examining table, shivering from pain and from a dim recollection of having been here before, Snowshoes made no attempt to get away.

He crouched, gazing up at Jerry.

"What happened?" the veterinarian asked. "Hit by a car?"

Incapable of answering, Jerry didn't try.

"Ah, well," said the vet. "Let's see what we have." He carefully palpated the furry body. "He's darn sore, but nothing's broken, far as I can tell. Tell you what. There's nothing much to be done for cats. They heal themselves. Or, of course," he said heartily, "they don't. But this fellow ought to be fine. Give him a warm corner and food and rest and he'll be right as rain in a few days."

Jerry, who could not think of a warm corner where Snowshoes would be safe, nodded.

Gazing down, the veterinarian said, "Seems to me I've seen this cat before. Those feet. Hmm." He shook his head. "Nope, can't remember. Dogs, now. I can tell one dog from another if I haven't seen them in—in a dog's age. Ha-ha. But cats all look alike."

"You're a sap."

"Oh, come on now."

"What do I owe you?"

"That's okay. I didn't do anything. Don't go away mad."

In the truck, Jerry sat for a long time, Snowshoes quiet on the seat beside him. Finally he leaned forward and started the motor.

"Only one thing I can think of to do, Snowshoes, my friend."

He drove slowly, several miles, across the river, to a big house outside a small town. He'd heard about Mr. and Mrs. Jaffee and their animal haven. Just about everybody around here had. He'd never expected to meet them.

M R. AND MRS. ARCHIBALD JAFFEE, who could probably have told one scorpion from another, so fond were they of all creatures great and small, lived outside a small town in a big house where they cared for wounded, unwanted, strayed, or abandoned animals.

Birds with broken wings or buckshot wounds. Cats and dogs hit by cars that did not stop. Pets adopted for the summer and discarded in the fall. Kittens who had turned into cats. Foxes and raccoons who had walked into traps. Lame horses, orphaned fawns, lambs rejected by their mothers, rabbits bought at Eastertime and grown troublesome by July.

To the Jaffees such as these were brought. Or, urged by instinct, some found their own way.

What had started long ago with a single instance of taking in a dog hit on the road and left to die (it hadn't) was now an occupation that absorbed all their days and found them by night filling out forms for the government. They were licensed to care for domestic animals and wild; pets and endangered species.

They had no complaints.

They nursed and protected their charges. If the animals had been pets and were healthy and attractive, new homes were found for them. An old or ugly creature that no one would adopt settled to live with the Jaffees for good. Wild creatures—fox or falcon or fawn, anything meant to fly or run free—were returned to the wild when they were well.

And where it was not possible to heal or to help, the Jaffees gently helped an animal to die.

Jerry pulled into the driveway and sat for a while, looking. Big old dilapidated house and barn. Big pasture, fenced, with chicken wire running between the posts so that it was entirely enclosed.

In there were a three-legged goat; some ducks shuffling across a shallow pond; a horse all bone standing at the fence with his heavy head drooping. Lying at the horse's feet was a fat homely dog with clouded eyes. A buzzard with one wing in a splint sat in the shade of a sugar maple. Several cats lounged on porch steps or railings. A small brown rabbit hopped across the matted lawn and made its way up the steps and through what was probably a cat door, cut in a dog door, cut in a regular door. Not a cat took notice of the rabbit.

The place breathed kindness. Safety.

A skinny woman shot out of the kitchen door like a cuckoo from a clock.

"Hi, there," she said to Jerry with a bright smile. "Looking for me?"

"You're Mrs. Jaffee?"

"That's me."

"I've—heard about you."

"Lots of people have. What've you got and where is it?"

"A cat. In my truck. He's—apparently he's been beaten. Or something."

"Oh, dear. Oh dear, oh dear. Will we need a blanket to wrap him in? Her?"

"Him."

"Is he frightened?"

"I guess not frightened. Just hurt. He won't make trouble."

Mrs. Jaffee tipped her head. "You say apparently. You don't know? He's not yours?"

"He . . ." Jerry hesitated. "No. Not mine. I found him by the road."

"I see."

He'd leave Snowshoes here as a waif, found by the roadside. Then the cat would have a chance at a new life, with no old reminders, not even a

name, to frighten him. Who knew how much an
animal remembered? Restored here to health, he
might forget altogether both Jerry's affection and
Roddy's malice.

No point in having a name to remind him. If
cats remembered.

In the kitchen, on a table covered with newspaper, Mrs. Jaffee handled Snowshoes with respectful
care and then said, "Nothing broken. I'll keep him
in the house for a while, give him a chance to mend
quietly. Cats are good at healing themselves."

"That's what the vet said."

"Oh? You took him to a veterinarian, did you?"

"It was on the way."

Mrs. Jaffee regarded him with clear affection.
"Will you be coming back for him?"

"No!" Jerry adjusted his glasses. "That's not—
convenient. The way I'm situated. No, you just do
what you can. Find him a new home, a good one.
You can do that?"

"No fear. The only homes we find for our animals are good ones. He's a young fellow, and probably a good-looker when he's feeling himself." She glanced down at Snowshoes, who hadn't moved. "He's polydactyl."

"Yeah? What's that?"

"*Poly*, many. *Dactyl*, digit. Many-toed. All four feet. That's unusual. I wonder what his name is."

"How do you know he has one?"

"This is a cat that's been cared for. Somebody's pet, no question of that, Mr.—ah?"

Jerry took some bills from his wallet. "Let me leave this. Pay for his keep."

"Goodness. That will more than pay for *his*."

"A contribution, then."

"Well, thank you so much. Let me give you a receipt. It's tax deductible, since we're a charitable organi—"

"No receipt," Jerry interrupted. "Just—see to him."

He put a hand softly on the cat's head, nodded two or three times, and walked out of the kitchen without saying good-bye.

"AND HE JUST WALKED OUT, without saying good-bye," Mrs. Jaffee said to her husband when he got home later in the day. He'd been making the rounds of bakeries, grocery stores, meat and fish markets, where the merchants gave him stale food and scraps for nothing.

Now he crouched to examine the black cat with the huge white feet who lay on his side in a big cushioned wicker dog basket that had been cradle to more creatures than either of the Jaffees could count.

"Wouldn't even say what this fellow's name is?"

"No. But he was awfully sad, leaving. That's his cat, all right. I wonder what could've happened?" She sighed. "Dearie me."

Mr. Jaffee shrugged. Unsolvable riddles didn't interest him. "No trouble placing this boy when he gets well. So—let's give him a name."

He took the brown rabbit onto his lap and waited for his wife to make tea before they had a conference. As the poet said, *The Naming of Cats is a difficult matter*.

Over tea and fruitcake they considered the difficult matter.

"It should have something to do with those twenty-four toes, don't you think?" said Mrs. Jaffee.

"They're a feature, all right."

"Poly, for polydactyl?"

"He'd be called Polly. He doesn't look like a Polly."

They went over some of the poet's suggestions. Mungojerrie and Rumpelteazer. Griddlebone. Firefrorefiddle, the Fiend of the Fell. Skimbleshanks and Bustopher Jones. Growltiger, The Terror of the Thames.

"They just aren't Vermont names," the Jaffees finally agreed. "He'd be hooted out of the state."

"There's Macavity," said Mrs. Jaffee. "*Macavity, Macavity, there's no one like Macavity*."

Mr. Jaffee shook his head. "Sounds like a toothache. Anyway, none of those have anything to do with his feet. Those paws *matter*."

The teapot was empty, the fruitcake crumbs, when they decided on Maximus. For maximum number of toes.

"Okay, then," said Mr. Jaffee, gently depositing the sleeping rabbit on the floor and addressing the cat in the basket. "Maximus. That's you. But I think we'll call you Max. How about something easy to eat? A dish of milk toast?"

By evening all the creatures had been seen to. Those in the barn, the pasture, and the house. Fed, petted, doctored, bedded down.

Max, who had painfully but greedily dispatched two bowls of milk toast, was back in the wicker basket, sharing it now with the rabbit. The rabbit was not Juniper, but Max found it good to lie again next to another furry being.

"I'm Mouse," said the rabbit.

"You look like a bunny."

"My *name* is Mouse."

"Funny name for a bunny."

"The children named me. They said I looked like a field mouse. That was when I was little. Last Easter."

"You aren't big now," said Max sleepily.

"Do you know why I'm not with the children anymore?"

"No, why?"

"*I* don't know why. I'm asking *you*."

"Children are funny, bunny. Mouse. Probably they got tired of you. I lived with some children once. They were nice. Anyway, mostly."

"Why aren't you still with them?"

Max didn't answer. He was thinking back, past

Jerry, to a hayloft, and a baby buggy, and a ski suit that was too small, and a dog that was too big lunging up and down in the snow. It was all too distant, too lost a time, to talk about.

"I'm sleepy," he said.

"Here's Cleopatra," said Mouse.

A fat, short-legged, near-blind dog waddled across the kitchen floor, stubby nails clicking. With a wheezy sigh she flopped beside the basket and peered into it. "Two of you," she gasped. "I can make out two of you in there. Is there room for me?"

"Of course," said Mouse. "Push over, Max. This is Maximus, Cleopatra. Max, for short. He just came today. He won't talk about it."

"That's all right," said Cleopatra. "I don't want to hear about it. Am I crowding you, Max?" she asked as she stumbled in, turning about two or three times, causing Max some pain. He didn't mind. It was all so cozy and kind.

"It's all right," he said. "I used to have a dog friend. Juniper. A border collie, he was. A working dog. I never worked, but we were friends anyway. We used to cuddle by the kitchen stove." The wind and the rain at the kitchen window . . . Juniper's rough coat . . . a bowl with CAT written at the bottom . . .

Nothing to talk about.

"I'm dachshund descended," said Cleopatra. "Some beagle, mostly dachshund."

"The Jaffees give all the creatures names when they come?" Max asked. "That's nice." But he wondered if he hadn't had too many.

"Not *all*," said Mouse. "Not the wild things. Only us animals that were pets."

"Aren't we pets now?"

Mouse considered. "I don't know. It's wonderful here, and I want to stay. But it's different from being just one pet with some people. I was in a house with a couple of cats and a dog, but I felt like a pet. Not part of a crowd. Happy crowd," she added. "And Cleopatra here had two people just to herself."

"What happened?" Max asked the dachshund.

"I've never been able to figure it out. I was riding with my people and all of a sudden I was in a ditch. I can remember wriggling in the air in my owner's hands, so he must've been trying to snatch me back. But—I still ended up in the ditch."

"What did you *do*?"

"Oh, I waited for them. For a long time. But they never found me."

"So you found this place?"

"Well, I got so hungry. I don't see very well, and I stumbled around in some fields for ages. But I got here," she said, sighing. "They—those people who owned me—they said I was fat and ugly, but I don't suppose that had anything to do with it."

"Of course not," said Max and Mouse together. Like all animals, they didn't care at all what another creature, beast or human, looked like.

The kitchen clock stood at midnight. Except for an occasional bark or whinny out of doors, or now and then the *whish* of the cat door or the dog door, there was silence.

In the wicker basket, Cleopatra snored and twitched. The little rabbit drowsed quietly, nestled next to Max, who slept and woke and slept again while his strength returned and the image of Jerry receded.

EXCEPT FOR THE BUZZARD with the broken wing and a bad-tempered one-eyed crow, wounded and baby birds were kept in large cages in the barn.

The barn was the first place where Max stopped for a few minutes every morning. He had healed quickly and liked to patrol the property for a while before going in for his morning nap.

Here he would sit, staring up at the cages with his great green eyes.

Most of the birds were too young, too hurt, or sufficiently aware of their safety behind the wire netting to pay cats much attention. But there were always a few that would flutter under that steady scrutiny. Max found all these wingy creatures attractive.

"Why do you suppose they flap and flutter like that?" he said one morning to an enormous marmalade cat, named Horace, who had joined him in studying the cages.

Horace, whose whiskers and tail tip were twitching, didn't reply, but Catherine, the crow, perching on a disused hay baler, squawked with scorn.

"Cats are asses!" she croaked.

"Cats are cats," said Max. "Asses are asses."

"You're a fool!"

"You're another."

"These poor little kin of mine are afraid of you, you *cat*."

"Why? I can't get at them."

"You would if you could."

"But I can't."

"They don't know that."

Max turned and regarded the crow. "You're a bird. Aren't you afraid of us?"

"Ha-ha-ha," said the crow hoarsely. "You take *me* on and you'll end up in fifty-six pieces on the barn floor. I could handle you with one wing tied."

Max was pretty sure this was true.

"Have you always been this disagreeable?" he asked curiously.

The crow ruffled her gleaming black feathers. "In my childwood I was rather nice, really."

"Child*hood*," Max corrected. He'd been around enough children to know that.

"I grew up in the woods," said Catherine. "So I had a childwood. Don't try to teach me how to talk."

"When did you go sour?" Max persisted.

"If you must know, it was when I got my eye shot out with a BB. I was flying around minding my own business—tormenting an owl—when this BB came from nowhere—"

"How could something come from nowhere?"

"It *came*," the crow said angrily, "from *I* knew not where. And it put out my eye. Probably would have put out my light, if Mrs. Jaffee hadn't been out tending to a sick lamb in the field and seen me fall."

"Are you cross with her?"

"I'm cross with everybody and everything. I'm entitled."

"I guess you are," said Max.

He walked out of the barn, tail high, to continue his patrol.

He pondered on the crow.

It seemed a terrible waste, to go on being so evil humored after something had happened that noth-

ing could be done about anyway. His own memory
was short, but he was aware that unpleasant things
had happened to him in his life, also short. The
difference between him and Catherine was that he
couldn't seem to recollect very clearly what those
things had been, or if they'd been so terrible after
all.

He sat under an apple tree in the orchard, washing and wondering. There was something about
tight and icy clothes. Had he ever actually worn
clothes? He, a cat, in rompers? Tight leggings?
Hadn't there been, too, a big dog slavering to get
at him, to rend him into fifty-six pieces as Catherine
had threatened to do? But the dogs around here,
all the dogs he'd ever known, were fine, just fine.
Maybe that monster had just been wanting to play?
And where had that been, anyway?

There had been a very mean boy, hadn't there?
Had there? Yes . . . somewhere there had been a
mean boy.

But all he could recall or care about, and that
in a secret sweet way that was more a feeling than
a true memory, were Juniper and Jerry.

He gave a final long lick down his chest, shook
his head to rid his tongue of some fur, and moved
off on his huge pads toward the pasture.

*   *   *

The horse always seemed to be in the same place, in the same position. Standing at the fence, big head hung over it, left front hoof curled under, tail swinging slowly.

"Are you as sad as you look?" Maximus inquired. He could be impertinent.

"I'm not sad at all," said the horse, whose name was Groundcover.

"Why do you look that way, then?"

"Can't help how I look. Can you help having feet the size of my hoofs?"

"No. But I was born with them. Were you born looking like the bottom of a barrel? They ought to call you Cloudcover."

The horse, instead of taking offense, took the opportunity to discuss himself with someone who actually seemed interested.

"I was a race horse. A trotter. That's why they called me Groundcover. And I could really cover it! Oh, those days, those days! The roar of the crowd! The cheers! The pounding hoofs! The wreath of carnations in the winner's circle!"

"You won a lot, then?"

"Well. In fact, I never won. Usually I brought up the rear, to be sure. But even the last horse across the wire has covered ground. You can see that."

"Stands to reason. But why do you remember the winner's circle so happily if you were never in it?"

"I saw it, didn't I? Oh, the wreath of carnations! The roar of the crowd!"

"Well, it sounds wonderful."

"It was." Groundcover lifted his head and gazed across the fields. "It was just that. Wonderful."

"What happened?"

"I suppose they decided I never would win a race, so they sold me for a hack."

"A hack?"

"A horse in a riding stable that any fool can rent

and ride. It breaks a horse, to have strangers on
his back all the time. Breaks his spirit. I didn't want
my spirit broken."

"Certainly not."

"So I threw a few people. Stopped suddenly. Ran
them under branches. Things like that."

"So then?"

"Then I was . . ." Groundcover's hide rippled.
"I was going to be put down."

"I see. So the Jaffees . . ." Max prompted.

"They heard about my plight and took me here,
and here I am. If I look sad, I suppose it's just
that I tend to dwell too much on past glories."

"You didn't have glory. You always lost."

"I didn't say *whose* glory I was dwelling on. Glory
generally—that's what I dwell on." He gazed down
at the cat. "Do I really look sad all the time?"

"You don't look merry."

"Must see what I can do about that," said
Groundcover. He turned and raced across the pasture. Showing, thought Max, beautiful form.

*   *   *

At the other side of the field was the place where the buzzard with the broken wing hung out. Every morning the male buzzard would appear and soar in narrowing circles until he landed, jagged wings held high, then furled as he hopped to his mate's side. He always brought something for her to eat. Usually a scrap of garbage. After she'd gulped it down, the two of them would remain side by side for a long time before he took off with a tremendous flapping that became, as he was airborne, an easy and elegant glide that took him up and up, away and away, until he was gone over the hills.

In the late afternoon, he would reappear and repeat the morning's pattern. One day, wing knitted and strong, she rose with her mate and they planed overhead for an hour or so before they disappeared over the hills for good.

So it went, at the Jaffees' shelter for creatures. One day followed another day. Animals came and went, were adopted or remained. Animals died, or went free.

Mouse and Max and Cleopatra slept together in the wicker basket every night and after a while could not remember a time when they had not.

THE JAFFEES, who were almost as fond of children as they were of animals, had had four daughters. Grown now. Married, with children of their own. The youngest, Joan Oliver, lived in a town ten miles away. She and her husband, Harry, had two daughters and a son. Neat, obedient children who seemed to be happy anyway.

One Saturday morning in October, a morning crisp and tangy as apples in the orchard, Mrs. Oliver arrived with her children for a day-long visit with her parents. A picnic was planned.

"I thought Harry was coming," said Mrs. Jaffee politely, though she hadn't thought so. Harry Oliver, except at Christmas and possibly Easter or the Fourth of July, avoided visits to his in-laws. He could not, he said, take all those animals. ("It isn't that I don't like them. I like kids, too, but I wouldn't want to live on a school bus.")

"You know how it is," Mrs. Oliver said to her mother. "Harry's always discovering something that needs to be done around the house. We found out that all those painted doorknobs are made of real brass. Beautiful. Imagine *painting* them."

"Mom says Daddy is house-proud," said Matty, the elder daughter. "She said it on the telephone to somebody."

"Matty, you don't have to repeat everything you hear."

"Well, you said it was all right if it wasn't carried too far."

"Just the same," said Mrs. Oliver, and then shrugged. She watched her mother tipping home-made doughnuts onto a paper plate, getting out a pitcher of lemonade made with lemons.

"How *do* you find time to cook the way you do, with all those creatures to take care of . . . ? Here, Mother, let me do that—"

She got a basket from the pantry, put a napkin in it, arranged the doughnuts neatly, talking all the while in a rather high voice.

"Yesterday," said Matty, "Mom told Daddy she wasn't even going to *notice* what a mess it is here or how it *smells*. I guess she's noticing. That's why she's talking that way."

"Matty!"

Unperturbed, Mrs. Jaffee said that she'd cooked this way when she had all her daughters to take care of.

"Mother, I *wish* you wouldn't speak as if children and animals were interchangeable."

"Aren't they?"

"No!"

"Oh. Well. Look, kiddies, we have an osprey in the barn. If you go very quietly, I think Grandpa will let you see him. Take your doughnuts with you."

Hank and Matty rushed off.

"Mind your clothes!" their mother called after them.

Emma, the youngest Oliver child, remained on the floor where she was, gently patting Cleo's head. She was six and had been tested for deafness because she rarely seemed to hear what people said. (She had not heard her mother ask her twice to please get up off the floor.) She was not, tests proved, deaf.

She just didn't hear what people said. Now she leaned over, crooning to Cleopatra, who shivered the length of her fat body with bliss.

Her mother, watching, shook her head and gave up. She said weakly, "I just hope Cleopatra hasn't been down in the woods playing what Harry calls pick-up-ticks."

"Tick season's over," said Mrs. Jaffee.

"Shall we go into the parlor?" said Mrs. Oliver, having arranged a tray to her satisfaction. "Come along, Emma."

Emma remained where she was.

In the parlor, Mrs. Oliver tipped Horace off a chair. "Do you *mind*?" she asked him, reversing the cushion. She examined it, sighed, and sat to pour lemonade. "What's wrong with the osprey?" she asked her mother.

A daughter of the Jaffees' could not be indifferent to the fate of hurt creatures. Mrs. Oliver liked animals. She simply did not want them leaving hair on her furniture or spots on her rugs.

"He was shot. By a sportsman," said Mrs. Jaffee.

"What?"

"The osprey. You asked about the osprey."

"Shot by one of those hunters? That's shocking."

"If shocking means surprising, no it isn't. What won't they shoot at? If it means horrible, wicked, yes . . . it's shocking."

"Will it be all right?"

"We hope so. We think so."

"Well, hunting season will soon be over, so *those* ticks will be gone, too, and maybe we can settle down to a long winter's peace."

Mrs. Oliver glanced around. Horace, turfed out of his chair, was sitting nearby waiting for a chance to reclaim it. There were two cats on the back of the sofa; a parrot named Jim Hawkins perched on a floor lamp; a young white cat was stretched on the window seat among pots of African daisies. Three or more cats sat on the windowsill outside looking in. A poodle named Valentine lay on a rug in one corner. He sighed a lot and gave off a musky odor.

Mrs. Oliver, sipping lemonade, observed it all resignedly, without comment.

"You're a nice girl," said her mother fondly, and they smiled at each other.

"Mama?" said a soft voice. "Mama, look."

Emma was in the doorway, inexpertly clutching a black cat with white feet. "Isn't he beautiful?"

A frown crossed Mrs. Oliver's features and was gone. "Yes, love. Beautiful. Now, put it down."

"No," said Emma, jerking her find close. The cat, draped all whichways in her arms, tipped his head back and stared at her.

"That's Max," said Mrs. Jaffee. "He's new."

"How can you tell?" her daughter asked sharply.

"Emma! Put that animal *down*."

"Look at all his *feet*," Emma said wonderingly. "He's got so many *feet*."

"That's why we named him Maximus, because he—"

"Emma!"

Emma began to howl. "I don't have no *pet*!" Her voice was aching.

"I don't have *any* pet," Mrs. Oliver said automatically.

"You don't *want* none!" Tears dripped on Max's head. He had made, so far, no move to escape.

"Any!" said her mother, and glanced at her own mother in exasperation.

"It is not natural for children to grow up without pets," Mrs. Jaffee began. "Certainly all you children had them—"

"We didn't ask for them. They were dumped on us."

Mrs. Jaffee laughed. "You loved them. Your sisters' children all have either cats or dogs. Or both."

"My sisters, every one, inherited *your* housekeeping skills."

"That sounds like a criticism."

"Just how it was meant to sound."

Mrs. Jaffee didn't take offense. "We were talking about pets—"

Emma listened. She could hear when her interests were touched upon. "All those cousins," she said. "They *all* have dogs. And cats." She sobbed. "Peter has white mice and two hamsters—"

"Last you heard, it was two," said Mrs. Oliver. She glared at her mother, who shrugged and nibbled a doughnut.

Matty and Hank came in with their grandfather. Considering their activities when they were with him, and his indifference to how messy they got, they were almost as tidy as when they'd run out. Grubby hands and knees, straw dust in their hair, but not bad, thought their grandmother.

"Run and wash up—" Mrs. Oliver began, and was interrupted by a bulletin from barn and pasture.

"Mother, the osprey is *beautiful*, even with his poor arm in a splint and you have to come out and see him and I *hate* hunters I'd shoot them *all* if—"

"Groundcover knows me! He wanted me to ride on him bareback, I could just *tell*, and he's looking real good—"

"Not *real* good," said their mother. "Really. Or just good. But not—"

"And there's about forty-nine dozen cats in the barn, some just bitty kitties, and why can't we—"

"Lookit," said Emma softly.

Her brother and sister, who'd been shouting, heard her at once.

Hank squatted next to her on one side, Matty on the other.

"Holy cow, look at those *tootsies*," said Hank.

"Listen to him purr," said Matty. "Like a sewing machine."

At that word, *tootsies*, Max stirred slightly, then closed his eyes again. Emma, holding him on her lap, sat on the floor with her back straight, legs stretched out before her.

And Mrs. Oliver looked at her three children,

absorbed in tenderness and wonder as they gazed at the sleeping cat.

"Of all animals, I think a cat . . ." She broke off, then resumed, "A cat is so self-contained, isn't it? No worrying about what to wear to the party, or whether the luggage will get lost, or why zucchini costs eighty-nine cents in the market when you can't *give* it away from the garden, or— They're so imper*turb*able. I envy them."

"You always did like cats," said Mrs. Jaffee. "Even as a baby, you—"

"I like all animals," Mrs. Oliver snapped. "I just don't want— Oh, well. Anyway, you know how Harry feels. I have *never* seen a cat before with feet like that."

"Polydactyl."

"Front *and* back."

"He's young. But not a kitten. It wouldn't be like training a kit—"

"Mother! Lower your voice!"

But the three children had turned and were regarding the two adults with anxious, hopeful eyes.

FROM HIS PERCH at the top of the floor lamp, Jim Hawkins shrieked, "Look at me look at me look at me!"

Max, sitting on a braided rug, washing his face, glanced up, one paw behind his ear. "I'm looking."

Jim Hawkins sidled down the lamp, swung to a ladderback chair, where he hung for a moment by his hooked bill before edging over to the back of the sofa. "Look at me look at me look at me!"

"I *said*. I'm looking."

Horace, comfortable now in his own chair, yawned. "He's parroting. Doesn't mean a thing. Just stuff he was taught to say when he worked in a roadside zoo. Say your other things, Jim."

"Hello, girlies. . . . Watch it, Mac. . . . Candy is dandy!" Jim Hawkins picked at the corner of a pillow he'd been working on for several days and lapsed into animal talk. "That's what I can remember. I forget the rest."

"No loss," said Horace.

"When I was employed, it was important. I hope nobody adopts me and wants me to learn all that stuff again."

The roadside animal act he'd been in had gone broke, and Jim Hawkins had been sold for twenty-five dollars to a customer who immediately got tired of him and left him with the Jaffees. No one so far had wanted to take him home. Apparently they did not find what he said interesting. He was not neat. He hated his cage, and unless it was covered screamed when he was put in it. He left droppings that had to be tidied up. He bit people. Nevertheless, he worried that someday someone would demand to adopt him.

"Why would anyone want you?" Horace said now. "You're about as sweet as a hatchet. You and that crow out there. Funny about birds," he went on, folding his paws beneath his chest. "Some of them are so adorable. A spark of chickadees—what could be more charming? But then you take birds like you and Catherine—"

"You'd rather take the chickadees," Jim Hawkins said nastily. "And we know how you want to take them. On the wing."

"Now you," said Horace, turning to Max, "are pretty sure to be adopted. Today."

Max felt his whiskers stiffen. "What do you mean?"

"Didn't you hear those children mooning and pleading?"

"Those children just now?"

"The very ones."

"They've gone away."

"They've gone on a picnic. When they get back, *if* I'm not mistaken, you'll be going home with them. Don't you listen when people are talking?"

"I was asleep. I was purring. I wasn't paying attention."

"Well, now you know."

"Why me? Why not you?"

Valentine, the old poodle, staggered up from his rug and came to join them, dragging one leg. He collapsed in front of Horace's chair.

"People don't adopt old animals," he said. "If they even look at me, which mostly they don't, they say goodness how old is *that* one. They say I smell. Do I? I mean, anything out of the ordinary?"

Max and Horace sniffed. "Smell all right to me," said Horace. "Me too," said Max.

"Just the same. And Horace here, he's too old, too. Of course, he can't do tricks."

Valentine flopped over on his side, legs stiff.

"Did he just die?" Max asked.

"Playing," said Horace. "He can play dead, and sit up, and if somebody puts a penny on the end

of his nose he can toss it and catch it in his teeth. What're some of your other tricks, Valentine?"

The poodle struggled upright.

"I used to be able to jump through a hoop. And I could wear a hat and walk around on my hind legs and give little hops. Can't, anymore. I'm not sure I could sit up, either."

He tried, waving his forepaws in the air, but had to steady himself on Horace's chair.

As the word tootsies had stirred a memory for Max, now Valentine's mention of wearing a hat stirred another. Sometimes on a dark night the wind will tear apart a cloud, revealing a star, immediately covered by another cloud racing by. Max's recollections of the past were like that. Winking into view, winking out. When, by chance or mischance, the past was summoned up in his mind, Juniper and Jerry shone brighter than stars. They were the moons of his memory, lost and glimpsed and lost again.

He teased at the notion of wearing a hat, then forgot as Mouse hopped into the room, followed by Cleopatra, puffing.

"We came to say good-bye," Cleopatra panted.

"Who to?" Max said crossly.

"You to," said Cleopatra. "Those children have been asking and asking to take one of us home. And now that woman *likes* you, Max. She says you have such interesting feet. And she says cats are nicer than any other animal."

"Funny thing to say," Valentine observed to Horace, who said why was it?

"Mouse and I were listening to them in the kitchen while they fixed their picnic," Cleopatra continued. "Fried chicken," she said dreamily. "And picnic eggs. And those cookies with nuts in them . . . Usually She remembers to give us a snack, but when those children are here—"

"Could you take me with you, Max?" Mouse asked softly. "Could I go on the adoption with you?"

"Of course you can."

"I want to go, too," said Cleopatra.

"If I'm going, so're you two," Max assured them.

Jim Hawkins, Horace, and Valentine exchanged glances.

"Put all three of your brains together," said the parrot, "and you couldn't get as high as stupid. Haven't you caught on about human beings yet?"

"I like them," said Cleopatra.

"You like our two, because our two are the best there are," said the parrot. "Maybe They would let an animal tell them what to do. If They were adopting Max here, they'd even figure *out* that Cleopatra and Mouse don't want to be separated from him. But They are different. There aren't any other human beings like ours."

"How do you know?" said Horace.

"Some of them are *very* nice," said Valentine.

Jim Hawkins shrieked.

"Are you two trying to say that other human beings are as good as ours?"

"We're saying *maybe* some are," Horace pointed out. "Stop screaming."

"Are you *saying*," Cleopatra asked Jim Hawkins, "that they won't let us go with Max?"

"Got it!" said the parrot. "*Exactly* what I'm saying. Watch it, Mac! Look out, girlies! Here come the Marines! *Hey*! That's another one. That was one of my sentences! I only just remembered—"

"Don't strain your brain remembering more," said Horace.

The white cat among the African daisies leaped to the floor. Rump in air, she stretched her front legs. Then, one at a time, her back legs. She, like the two silent cats on the sofa back, was a stray who had somehow found her way to the Jaffees and had settled down with them.

Her name was Eleanor.

She looked at Max, Mouse, and Cleopatra. "I don't understand," she said, "animals who think they have any say about anything, where human beings are concerned."

She walked from the room, tail high. The two silent cats on the sofa got down and followed, leaving Max, Mouse, Cleopatra, Jim Hawkins, Horace, and Valentine to paw over the matter of adoption.

They arrived at no conclusion.

The conclusion was taken care of by Mrs. Oliver and her children, who drove off through the spice-colored hills late in the afternoon with Max, wide-eyed and subdued, on Emma's lap. During the drive, Mrs. Oliver gave instructions. They had wanted the cat, therefore the cat was their responsibility, which they were to take turns at without shirking. Feeding, fresh water, brushing every day,

litter pan changed each day (Max was to be an in-
door cat until he knew enough not to run away),
and proper attention paid *in every way.*

"Otherwise, back he goes."

Shouts of protest.

"Children! This is going to be difficult enough.
You know your father . . ."

Silence. And then, "We'll take care of him,
Mama," said Emma.

"Sure we will," her brother and sister agreed.

Harry Oliver was happily gloating over his newly
furbished front door. Overhead fanlight window
sparkling. Locks, knob, hinges, and a knocker in
the shape of a fox's head, shining in their original
brass beauty.

As his family turned into the driveway, he
bounded down the steps to greet them. "Ah! Back
from the animal fair! The birds and the beasts were
there? Why do I ask? Just come and see what I've
done—inside and out not a painted doorknob or
hinge to be seen. Regard, I ask you, that front door,
regard—"

"Harry," his wife interrupted nervously. "Harry,
listen. We've got a little surprise for you."

O F COURSE, THE OLIVER CHILDREN wanted to name their own special absolutely first pet of any kind. There was much consulting lists of real names; and consideration of names of countries ("How about India? India Oliver, that's neat"); names of towns ("We could name him Mary Meyer, Vermont. And call him Mary for short," Matty suggested, to Hank's horror); some just silly names (Sticklepad, Splatfoot, Picklepuss, Jelly); and some quite nice names (Merrycat. Or, simply, Oliver). They decided on Mistletoes.

"That's because he's better than a Christmas present," Emma explained to her parents at breakfast.

"And it takes his feet into account," Hank pointed out.

Matty eyed her father uneasily. "Isn't that a nice name, Daddy?"

"I don't care if you name him Meow Tse Tung, just see that he stays outdoors or in the mudroom." The mudroom, off the kitchen, was where they hung their jackets and left their boots before coming into the house.

Emma burst into tears, as she'd been doing regularly since Mistletoes had arrived with them on the weekend. It was now Thursday.

"That's not *fair*," Hank protested. "He's our *pet*. Pets don't get shoved outdoors or into mudrooms all the time. Pets share with the people. Besides, he can't go outside by himself. He isn't used to the house yet."

"We put butter on his paws, to make him stay," said Matty. "I read about that. They lick off the butter and that makes them feel at home, because they've washed and had something to eat at the same time."

"Where did it take place, this buttering?" Mr. Oliver demanded.

"In the mudroom, of course," said his son. "*On* newspaper. I don't think butter on my feet in a mudroom on newspaper would make me feel at home."

"I remind you. I did not ask for this pet. I was not consulted. I get asthma from cat dander. I don't want hair all over the house and the furniture clawed and—and that's final."

"But Harry," said Mrs. Oliver, "he's really such a lovely clean animal. We can brush him every day—I mean, the children will—and he's perfectly housebroken. We'll give him a scratching post. And you don't get asthma. You have a slight cold and it just coincided, that's all."

"We *never* have a pet," Matty sniffled. "*Every*body else has pets. But not us. And now we can't even *see* ours. It isn't fair—"

Mr. Oliver put his napkin down, rose from the table, and said, "I have to be going. If you kids want me to drop you at school, get cracking. You've already missed the bus."

Dressed for school, the children had been in the mudroom trying to reassure Mistletoes that pretty soon he'd be allowed in the house like a regular pet, when the school bus had passed. Now it was either ride with their father, or walk and be late.

In a sullen row in the backseat, they were driven to school, unspeaking.

" 'Bye, kids," said their father as they climbed out of the car.

They marched off, not turning to wave as they usually did.

"Damn," said Mr. Oliver and slapped the steering wheel.

In a hayloft long ago, this black cat with big white feet had thought it would be nice to have a name of his own. Now he'd had several, and he was only a year and a half old.

Alone in the mudroom, lying on a sleeping bag provided for him, he licked his paws and tried to recall all his names. He could remember only Max.

Having a name, even having a lot of names, didn't seem as wonderful as once he had thought it would be. Probably—he spread his claws and delicately nibbled between them—the best thing would be to have just *one* name.

That way a creature would know who he was. Whose pet he was.

He stopped washing, one hind foot in the air beside his ear, eyes fixed on space. For a long time he remained motionless while his small bright brain pursued a thought to its hole. Just before it dove into darkness, he caught it, as he would catch a mouse.

Perhaps his mother had been right. *It was better not to have a name, and not to be a pet.*

He toyed with this notion, shaking it, tossing it

about, securing it under his paw. Then he let it
go, as sometimes he let a mouse escape.

He was not like his mother and his sister and
his brother. He liked being a pet. He liked human
laps and voices. He liked his food to be cooked.

What he did not care for was being whisked away
from Mouse and Cleopatra and the Jaffees. He did
not want to be all alone in a mudroom.

Each day since he had been there, the children
had eaten their breakfast and departed. After, to
be sure, a brief visit to him in his confinement.
The man left the house without paying a call on
the cat. When they were gone, the woman went
about cleaning and cleaning, then talking on the
telephone about which meeting she was going to
today. She'd look into the mudroom and say something silly like "Behave yourself, Mistletoes." Or
"Don't go away."

She'd check to be sure the children had given
him food and fresh water and cat crackers. That
they'd cleaned his pan.

Then she'd drive off. Leaving Mistletoes to silence and to sleep.

What else, but sleep?

There was no sound in the room off the kitchen,
and very little light. Boots and umbrellas were lined
up along one wall; jackets hung from hooks; a neat

arrangement of mops and brooms and pails stood against another wall. Never in his life before had Mistletoes been in a place so clean, so soundless.

It was true that late in the day the children came in to visit him and pet him and throw a little ball across the floor for him to chase. When a great many days had passed, they began to take him outside—*on a leash*—for a tiny walk after dinner.

Then, until morning, he'd be alone in the mud-room again with nothing but his paws to keep him company.

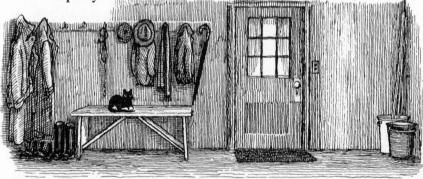

He had had too many names, too many homes in his short life. He could not keep a clear image of it all. He recalled certain figures, certain voices, as through a shining mist. There were other, murky, pictures that he closed his mind against.

But the time at the Jaffees' house, recent and cloudless, tugged at him now, teased him with longing, as he lay alone licking his paws.

*   *   *

The Oliver children were truly fond of their cat. But children have busy lives.

Hank was a basketball player with Olympic aspirations. Hours of his day went into practice. What time was left went for homework, chores, eating, and sleeping. With no other slot to slip him into, Mistletoes became a chore.

Matty spent her time cutting, pinking, trimming, embroidering the fabrics of her daydreams. She wouldn't neglect their new pet, their only pet that they'd ever had, sweet Mistletoes. He just kept slipping through the chinks of her attention.

Emma was fondest of him. Emma really loved him. But she was in her first year of real school and was nervous about it. Besides, she hated sitting in the mudroom, and their father wouldn't let Mistletoes in the house.

Mistletoes, who continued to think of himself as Max, did not feel well and warmly welcomed.

THE JAFFEES SAT in their parlor one winter evening watching Jacques Cousteau watching
whales from the deck of *Calypso*.

Mouse and Cleopatra had gone to bed in their
basket. Valentine lay at Mr. Jaffee's right foot, whif-
fling in his sleep. Ben, a new dog, sat upright at
his left foot. One of the silent cats, Pearl, slept on
Mrs. Jaffee's lap, and Jim Hawkins, who grew
quieter as the day wore on, sat on a cushion picking
at a bit of fringe he'd overlooked till now.

The telephone rang.

"Mother," said Mrs. Oliver, "do you think this
cat will come back? It's gone, and we can't find it
and we've looked everywhere and called and
called. . . . The children are beside themselves—"

At an inquiring look from her husband, Mrs. Jaffee said, "Max—I mean Mistletoes—is missing."
Then, into the phone, "How long has he been
gone?"

"Since night before last. I waited, thinking surely

he'd come back, but now . . . What's that, Harry?
Oh. Harry says it should be spelled *Missile*toes,
Mother. Spelled m-i-s-s-i-l-e. His little joke . . . Of
course, Harry's the only one the cat has scratched.
Yet."

"That's odd. He never scratched while he—"

"Now don't go blaming Harry. He was just trying to put it back in the mudroom. The children
had let it into the house, and it *was* clawing the
furniture. You said it wouldn't. Harry just picked
it off the couch, that's all."

Holding him firmly, very firmly, Mrs. Jaffee
imagined, wondering how she and her husband had
brought up a daughter who'd call an animal *it*.

She said, "Why do you say the children had let
him in the house? Where is he usually?"

"Oh, Mother . . . don't. It's all difficult enough
without lectures from you."

"Where has the cat been staying?"

"It—"

"He."

"All right, of course. He has been left mostly
in the mudroom because we're gone all day practically and I can't have litter pans in the house, can
I? And he does claw the furniture, so if he was
in here—"

"How did he happen to get away?"

"I told you. Harry was putting him back in the

mudroom, but one of the children had left that door open. It's actually their fault, the whole thing, but they feel so awful I can't say anyth—"

"You really shouldn't have a pet. That's what I've decided. It isn't your *fault* that you put cleanliness above goodliness—"

"Mother!"

"Sorry. But animals really don't fit into the scheme of things for you and Harry."

"But the children wanted it—wanted Mistletoes so badly. You saw that. You're the one who's always saying children need a pet."

"Well, I don't know what to tell you about this. Cats do go off for a few days sometimes, and come back. Let's hope Mistletoes is just—will be back soon."

"If he isn't, in a few days we'll come and get a short-haired dog, if you have one. Harry's finally agreed to let the children have a pet. They're *broken*-hearted about Mistletoes, but rather excited at the idea of a dog. Except Emma."

"If," said Mrs. Jaffee coldly, "you got this short-haired dog—which we don't happen to have one of," she said, looking at Ben, who had short hair, "what will you do if the pet you already have should try to come home to you?"

"Oh, dear. Well, we'll worry about that when the time comes."

"Please do let us know if the time comes, so we can worry too."

"Well, you don't have to sound so sarcastic."

When she'd hung up, Mrs. Oliver said to her husband, "Mother's upset. Maybe I shouldn't have told her."

"Where animals are concerned," said Harry Oliver, "both your parents are hanging off their hinges."

"I suppose." She sighed. "I wish that animal would come back."

"So do I," her husband lied.

Mrs. Jaffee, picking up Pearl and sitting down again, stared at her husband for a while. "Where do you suppose he is?" she said at length.

Mr. Jaffee shook his head.

"Now she says they'll get a short-haired dog for the children."

"Not from here, they won't."

"She should know that it's wrong to have a pet when people are gone all day. *And* when the house can't take a little mussing up. I should have known better. Poor Max. I should *never* have let them take him. My fault, entirely."

Mr. Jaffee put a hand on Ben's fine head. "Maybe he'll come back here to us."

"Ten miles—maybe more—of unfamiliar ter-
rain?"

"It's been known to happen. At least, you read
where cats travel incredible distances. Gone for
months and then turn up on the old doorstep asking
for breakfast as if they'd never been away."

"If you believe stuff like that."

"I tend to believe good stuff like that. So do you."

"Maybe."

To a background of humpback whales singing,
Mrs. Jaffee thought about a black cat with big white
paws wandering through the frigid night, probably
hungry, certainly uncertain of where he was. Could
he protect himself from raccoons or hostile dogs?
Would he know enough to watch out for cars?
Would he find places to shelter from the cold, from
storms when they came? Would he find a home
somewhere—cats were expert at that—or at least
manage to feed himself?

"Come on," said her husband. "Listen to the
whales singing."

They sang, way off in the Pacific Ocean, each
to each. Whales were threatened with extinction.
One way or another, all creatures on the planet
were so threatened, including man himself. By man
himself.

In a world so filled with peril to animal and man
alike, it seemed silly to worry about one small cat

who in the end could probably take care of himself. He'd known where he didn't belong. With luck, he'd find someplace where he did.

Mrs. Jaffee told herself this, and listened to the whales singing, and worried about one cat.

CATS ARE NOT HIKERS, and it takes a real predicament to put one on the road.

When Tootsy-Wootsy, in his pink-and-purple ski suit, had dashed away from the farmer's daughter, he had not been thinking. He'd been trying to run out of his clothes. Once across the highway, he'd had no choice but to go on.

And so it had been with the mudroom. Mistletoes, seeing his chance to escape, took it with no thought of what came next. Once well away, he stopped running and began to walk.

He had no direction in mind. Jerry and the Jaffees swam in the bright mist of his good memories. Juniper and Cleopatra and Mouse were there, glimpsed and lost sight of, glimpsed again. He did not know if he was going toward any of them.

Where were they now? Where had they ever been?

He walked.

He got hungry.

He kept walking.

In summer, in bird- and mouse- and rabbit-haunted pastures, even an inexperienced cat could contrive to eat. But on the frost-hard dirt roads and meadows he now traversed day after day, he just kept from starving.

He forgot his name.

He tried to get adopted.

Once, at a country inn, he thought he had a chance. A kindhearted cook fed him at the kitchen door for a couple of days. He ruined things by creeping inside to sit by the fire. Another cat, a huge Maltese named Anna, already owned the inn and the fire. She did not mind having another cat fed—outside. Inside was her territory, and she had never learned, like the animals at the Jaffees', to share. She had not the faintest intention of sharing.

The black cat had scarcely made it to the hearth before the air was full of fur. His. Anna chased him outdoors and beat him up in the yard.

Sick and aching, he finally got free of her and limped down the road until he found a hollow stump to crawl into. He lay there for three days, licking several deep wounds, sleeping with his paws over his nose to keep it warm.

Weeks later, at a country grocery store, his sense of hope, which had leaked almost entirely away,

began to rise again. There was a gas pump in front
of the store, and the gas pump put him in mind
of a person, a place, a time when he had been happy.

Warily, he mounted the wooden steps in front
of the grocery store, leaped to a windowsill, and

looked in. It was night, and the store was closed. One light at the back shone on shelves and counters. Getting under a rocking chair left on the porch, he waited in the cold that was not quite as cold as it had been.

Early in the morning Mr. Scourby arrived, parked at the side of his store, walked up the steps flipping through his keys. He was at the door when he saw the cat, who gazed up at him, not moving.

"Well, well," said Mr. Scourby. "Been waiting long?"

The cat came out from under the chair and wound himself around Mr. Scourby's legs, butting his head against them. His purring machine, long disused, began to throb.

Mr. Scourby leaned over and scratched behind the cat's ears. "You've been having a time of it, haven't you?" he said. "Hungry, I suppose. Wait here, boy."

The cat was finishing a dish of canned food, gobbling frantically, when Mrs. Scourby arrived in their old station wagon.

"Wait!" her husband called. "Don't let Maggie out!"

Too late.

Maggie, an old, amiable, very big, highly curious black Labrador, was already out of the wagon and loping forward to investigate. As she bounded up the steps, the cat streaked off the porch, across a churchyard, and out of town.

Mr. and Mrs. Scourby and Maggie watched his flight rather sadly.

"Poor thing," said Mrs. Scourby. "Lost, I guess."

"Yup. Been having a time of it, that one. Skinny and beat up and scared to death." He leaned over and tugged gently at Maggie's ear. "Doesn't know friend from foe. Right, old girl?"

Maggie, who would have accepted that cat and forty more like him, waved her tail and forgot him.

BROOKS AND RIVERS splintered their coats of ice and began to run freely. A few beavers emerged and set to work impeding the flow of smaller streams. Up came skunk cabbage, fiddler ferns, jack-in-the-pulpits, and out came buds along the boughs. Peepers had yet to arrive, but the days lengthened and warmed. Imperceptibly. Steadily.

There was a lot of mud.

The cat by now was wild enough to have astonished even his mother, if she'd remembered him. (She would not have. She was occupied in the hayloft with a new set of kittens. None polydactyl, and none with dreams of setting up as a house cat.)

He had had more fights, but was getting better at it. He'd been chased by a few dogs and chased off a few in turn, and he now knew a better way to get out of a tree than falling off a branch.

Once he tangled with a raccoon, and lost. But most of the wounds this time were on his rump. He had learned when to stand and fight, and when

to run away. He'd become a good hunter, and the
pads of his paws were tough from walking.

Some days he walked a lot. Sometimes, for days,
he scarcely made any progress, which was all right
since he did not have progress in mind.

No goal anymore. Few memories, and those
blurred. Glimmers of recollections that flickered
and dimmed. He would have answered to no name.
Or, in fact, to any name, had there been someone
to call him one.

He avoided towns and houses, places where human beings and watchdogs and cats with territorial rights were found. He lived in meadows, beside streams, now and then ventured into the woods.

He survived.

One day in June—his second birthday if he'd known—he lay on a stone wall warmed by the sun. He was half asleep when a little red fox trotted by, stopped, one misshapen foot tucked against his white chest.

"Hello, Cat," he said.

"Hello—Dog?"

"Fox."

"Oh. Fox."

"What are you doing?"

"Sitting on this wall."

The fox sat down, lowered his foot to the ground, stared up. "You *live* out here?"

"I don't think I live anywhere."

"I've seen plenty of cats. But they *usually* dwell in barns. Or houses."

The cat thought back. "You're right. That's where they usually dwell. *We* usually dwell. What's the matter with your foot?"

"Nothing now. Not anymore. But I was caught in a trap."

"How did you get out?"

"It was *most* strange. A man came along after I'd been there—a long time. I was trying to gnaw my foot off to escape, but that man came up to me and he *opened the jaws of that trap.* Do you believe it?"

"Yes," the cat said, reflecting. "Yes . . . I guess I do."

"I tried to bite him."

"Naturally."

"I was too weak. I could only snap. I missed."

"Then what?"

"Let me tell you, Cat . . . that man pulled that trap *out* of the ground and *carried* it and me back to a human habitation—a house, mind—"

"I remember."

"And he *broke* that trap to bits! This woman there *washed* my foot in warm water and *wrapped* something soft around it—"

"A bandage," said the cat.

"How do you know?"

"I just remember."

Something was fretting at the cat's lazy, sun-warmed soul. A call, a summons. He did not know how to answer.

"Then what?" he said again to the fox.

"Then I stayed there with those human beings. Not in the house, *their* house. In an old goat house. My foot got better and better and they *fed* me and there were a lot of creatures around, *all* kinds, and I was thinking of settling down with them but they didn't want me."

"People generally don't," the cat said. He did not sound bitter. He did not sound as if he entirely believed his own words. Maybe, he said to himself,

his sluggish mind beginning to move a mite faster, maybe some people want animals around them and some don't.

Could be.

The way some animals want human beings around them and some don't.

The way I don't, he said to himself. The way I *do?*

"That's not how it was," the fox went on. "This man and this woman, *they* said that wild animals, after they've mended from whatever hurt them, should go back to the wild. *And* they shouldn't get to trust human beings or be fond of them because *then* when they're back in the wild they might trust the wrong ones. *That's* why I never got into the house, with the dogs and the cats and the animals with names. Anyway, that's what the *horse* told me. I guess he should know. He's been there a *long* time."

The cat sat up, whiskers, ears, his very fur alert.

"What was this horse's name? Did he have a name?"

"All the animals on the *human* side had names. Just not us wild ones. There were three baby raccoons"—the fox licked his lips—"and a couple of owls, *and* a deer. They've had that *deer* since he was orphaned last year and they're trying to *make* him go back to the wild and he just won't

do it and it worries them a *lot*, at least that's what
the *horse* said—"

"What was the horse's name?"

The fox blinked. "It's been a while. Let's see . . .
Groundhog—"

"Groundcover," said the cat, getting to his feet.
"Is this place far?"

"From where?"

"From here."

The fox tipped his head, listening to a rustle in
the ivy on the wall. Chipmunk? He darted at a chink
in the stones, sat back to listen again.

"The place where they fixed your foot," said the
cat. "Is it far? From here? Which direction?"

The fox decided that if there had been a chipmunk, it had gone to ground. He gave his attention
back to the cat.

"Not far. Over there, through that little woods
at the top of the hill, on the other side of the pasture
that's on the other side of the hill. . . ." He spoke
distractedly, listening to the wall.

The cat jumped to the ground and started off.

"I'll bet this wall is *full* of chipmunks," the fox
was saying. "Plenty for both of us. Where are you
going?"

"Home," said the cat and began to trot on his
big feet. He held his tail high. "I have a name,"
he called back. "It's *Max*!"

He arrived late at night in the moonless dark and stood for a while on the back porch, not thinking, only conscious of being back and belonging. A summer wind trampled the treetops. There was the fluttering call of a screech owl, bark of a barred owl. A dog on a distant farm howled briefly. A toad flopped out of the garden onto the path and was immediately covered by the barred owl, who silently carried it off.

Max turned and went through the cat door, made his way across the dark kitchen to the wicker basket.

He moved soundlessly, but Mouse sensed his presence. She woke and said, "Max! It's you! Where have you been? What've you been doing?"

"Is there room for me in there?"

"Of course. Cleopatra!" Mouse said loudly. "Cleopatra, push over! Max is back! She's deaf now, Max, and can't see at all anymore, but she'll be glad you're back, when she figures it out. Cleopatra!"

When they were finally adjusted together in the basket, Mouse said again, "What *have* you been doing?"

Max considered. "Nothing much. Just coming home. To my friends."

"You've been a long time about it."

"Yes. But here I am."

"That's what counts," said Mouse contentedly.

THE END